Presented to

_____

By

_____

On

_____

For Sheila and Bethany.
–D.S.

To my mom. I love you.
–S.B.

ZONDERKIDZ

The Sweetest Story Bible
Copyright © 2010 by Diane M. Stortz
Illustrations © 2010 by Sheila Bailey

Requests for information should be addressed to:

Zonderkidz, *Grand Rapids, Michigan 49530*

Library of Congress Cataloging-in-Publication Data
Stortz, Diane M. –
    Sweetest Story Bible / by Diane Stortz ; [Sheila Bailey, illustrator.].
         p.   cm.
    ISBN 978-0-310-71673-0 (hardcover)
    1. Bible stories, English. 2. Girls—Religious life. I. Bailey, Sheila. II. Title.
    BS551.3.S77 2009
    220.9'505—dc22   2008053936

Editors: Barbara Herndon and Doris Rikkers
Creative direction: Kris Nelson
Art direction and design: Jody Langley

Printed in China

10 11 12 13 14 15 /SCC / 6 5 4 3

Sweet Thoughts and Sweet Words for Little Girls

The Sweetest Story Bible

Written by Diane Stortz   Illustrated by Sheila Bailey

ZONDERkidz

ZONDERVAN.com/
AUTHORTRACKER
follow your favorite authors

Table of Contents

From the
Old Testament

From the
New Testament

Old Testament

The Lord your God is with you. He is mighty enough
to save you. He will take great delight in you.
The quietness of his love will calm you down.
He will sing with joy because of you.

–Zephaniah 3:17

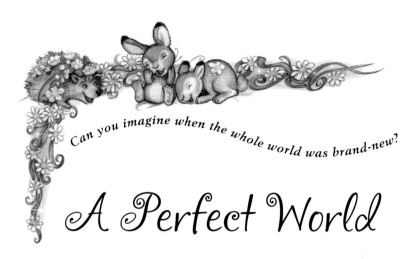

Can you imagine when the whole world was brand-new?

A Perfect World

Genesis 1 – 2

*L*ong ago, nothing existed except God—no sky, no earth, no grass, no animals, no people. But God is love, and he had a loving plan. In the beginning, God created the heavens and the earth.

On the first day, God said, "Let there be light," and light shone all around! God called the light *day*, and he called the darkness *night*.

On the second day, God said, "Let there be sky." Suddenly brilliant blue sky floated high above the earth!

"Let the water gather in one place," God said, "and let there be dry ground." Sure enough, the seas formed and the land popped up! Then God told plants and grass and trees to burst from the land, and they did. This was the third day.

Then God spoke again. On the fourth day, he made the sun, the moon, and the stars, and on the fifth day, all fish and birds. On the sixth day, God made all animals. *Everything* God made was good.

The next part of God's plan came on the sixth day too. God said, "Let us make people in our image, to take care of the earth and rule over it." God created a man and a woman, Adam and Eve. They loved each other, and God loved them both.

God's sweet story had begun, and it was *very* good!

Sweet Thought
God thought of you when he made the world!

Sweet Words
I am the Lord. I have made everything.

– Isaiah 44:24

13

Have you ever felt sad when something good was gone?

A Sneaky Snake

Genesis 2 – 3

God planted a garden with beautiful trees that gave delicious fruit. "Live here in the garden," God told Adam. "Take care of it." So Adam lived in the garden with Eve, his wife.

Two special trees grew in the garden, the tree of life and the tree of knowing good and evil. God told Adam, "You may eat the fruit of any tree *except* the tree of knowing good and evil. Don't eat the fruit from that tree."

A sneaky snake, God's enemy, hissed at Eve one day, "Why don't you try the fruit on the tree of knowing good and evil? If you do, you will know everything, just like God."

The fruit on the tree looked yummy, and Eve
wanted to be like God. So she ate some. She gave
some to Adam, who was with her, and he ate some too.

What a *big* mistake! Now Adam and Eve knew about evil. They had spoiled God's perfect world.

"Even though you hate the people I made," God told the sneaky snake, "my sweet story will not end."

But God sent Adam and Eve out of the garden and guarded the way to the tree of life with a flaming sword.

Sweet Thought
God's commands
are always right.

Sweet Words
Your word is like a lamp
that shows me the way.

–Psalm 119:105

What do you like to do on a rainy day?

Safe in a Big Boat

Genesis 6 – 9

Noah loved God and always tried to obey him. No one else loved God or obeyed God like Noah did.

"Build a big boat," God told Noah. "I'll tell you how. Make rooms inside for many animals. Paint tar inside and outside so the boat won't leak. Put a door on one side. I'm sending a flood, but I will keep you safe in the big boat—you, your family, and two of every kind of animal!"

Noah built the big boat. He stored food on board for his family and the animals. He did everything just as God told him.

Then God said, "It's time!" Noah and his family went in the boat. So did the animals God sent to Noah, two by two. When everyone was inside, God closed the door.

First a *drip*, then a *drop*, then a *drip-drop, whoosh!*—the rain began. For forty days and forty nights, the rain poured down, but inside the boat everyone stayed safe and dry.

Finally the rain stopped. Slowly the water dried up. God told Noah, "It's time to leave the big boat." Noah and his family came out first and then the animals, two by two.

"Thank you for taking care of us!" Noah told God.

"I will always take care of you," God said. He promised never to flood the earth again. He made the rainbow to remind everyone of his promise.

Sweet Thought
God keeps us safe!

Sweet Words
We trust in the Lord
our God.
– Psalm 20:7

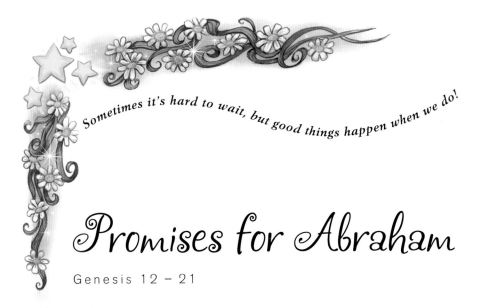

Sometimes it's hard to wait, but good things happen when we do!

Promises for Abraham

Genesis 12 – 21

"Pack up!" God told Abraham. "Go to the land I will show you. I'm going to make you a great nation. I'm going to bless you and use you to bless others."

Abraham folded up his tents and packed all his belongings. He traveled to the land of Canaan with his servants, all his sheep and goats, and Sarah, his wife. "All this land will belong to you someday," God said. "I will give this land to your children and to their children."

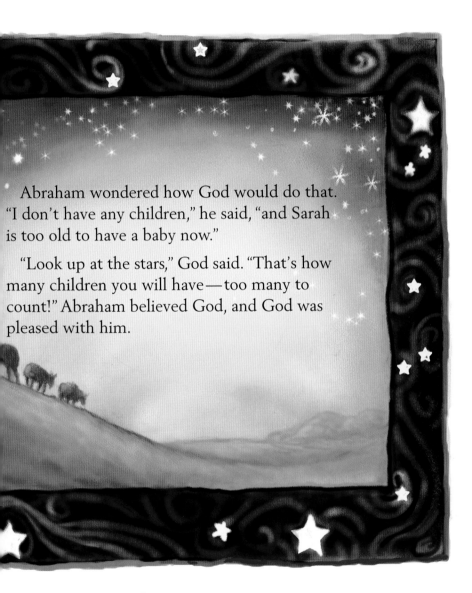

Abraham wondered how God would do that. "I don't have any children," he said, "and Sarah is too old to have a baby now."

"Look up at the stars," God said. "That's how many children you will have—too many to count!" Abraham believed God, and God was pleased with him.

When Abraham was ninety-nine, God told him, "Sarah will have a baby boy about this time next year. Name him Isaac. Everything I've promised you, I will promise Isaac also."

Later, when she heard the news, Sarah laughed. But God's sweet promises always come true! Baby Isaac arrived just when God said he would. Sarah laughed again because she was so happy!

Sweet Thought
God does what he says he will do!

Sweet Words
The One who promised is faithful.
– Hebrews 10:23

How exciting it is when a princess meets her prince!

A Wife for Isaac

Genesis 24

"Go to my homeland," Abraham told his servant. "Find a wife for my son Isaac. God will guide you."

Abraham's servant went to the land where Abraham's relatives lived. He stopped at a well and prayed, "Dear God, I will ask a young woman to give me a drink. If she gives a drink to me and to my camels as well, I will know she is the one for Isaac."

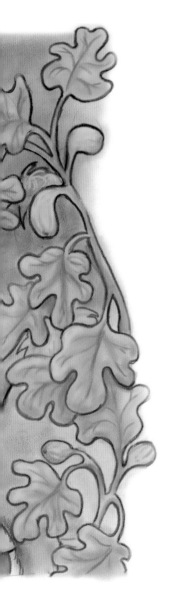

Beautiful Rebekah came to the well with her water jar. "Please give me a drink," said Abraham's servant.

"Certainly, sir!" said Rebekah. "I'll get water for your camels too!"

When the camels finished drinking, Abraham's servant gave Rebekah a gold ring and two gold bracelets. "What is your father's name?" he asked.

"My father is Bethuel," Rebekah answered.

"Praise the Lord!" said the servant. "He has led me straight to Abraham's relatives!"

Rebekah ran to tell her family what had happened. The family spoke to Abraham's servant. Then they asked Rebekah, "Do you want to marry Isaac?"

"Yes, I will go," Rebekah said.

When Rebekah saw Isaac walking in the fields, she got off her camel and asked Abraham's servant, "Who is that?" It was Isaac! Rebekah shyly covered her face with her veil.

Soon Rebekah married Isaac. They loved each other very much.

Sweet Thought
God knows what we need.

Sweet Words
I will make a helper who is just right for him.
– Genesis 2:18

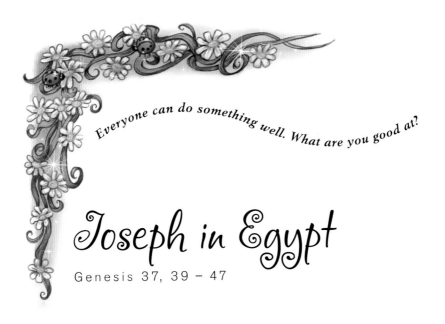

Everyone can do something well. What are you good at?

Joseph in Egypt

Genesis 37, 39 – 47

Isaac's son Jacob had twelve sons. God gave one of them, Joseph, special dreams. But Joseph's older brothers were jealous and disliked him, so they sold him to traders traveling to Egypt. What a terrible day!

The traders sold Joseph as a servant to a man named Potiphar. God cared for Joseph and blessed his work. Soon Potiphar put Joseph in charge of all he owned.

But Potiphar's wife, a grumpy lady, got Joseph in trouble with her husband, even though Joseph had done nothing wrong. So Potiphar sent Joseph to jail. Poor Joseph!

But God cared for Joseph and blessed his work. Soon Joseph was in charge of the jail!

Another prisoner in the jail had been the king's chief wine taster. One night the man had a dream that worried him. "God can tell me the meaning of your dream," Joseph said. Joseph's answer pleased the wine taster. "When you get out of jail, please help me get out too," Joseph said. But the wine taster forgot.

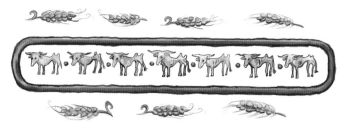

Later Pharaoh, the king, had a dream no one could understand. Finally the wine taster remembered Joseph! Joseph told Pharaoh the meaning of his dream. "For seven years, no food will grow," he said. "Find the wisest man in Egypt and put him in charge. Have him store up grain now so everyone will have enough to eat later."

"Because God has told you these things," said Pharaoh, "you are the wisest man in Egypt. I am putting you in charge."

Joseph's brothers came to Egypt to buy grain. They met Joseph, but they didn't know it was him. "I am your brother!" cried Joseph. "You meant to hurt me when you sold me as a slave, but God sent me here to keep you alive!"

Jacob, his sons, and all their families soon moved to Egypt to be near Joseph and to have enough food. They lived in Egypt a very long time and were called the Israelites.

Sweet Thought
God gives us talents to use for him!

Sweet Words
We serve God in every way.
– 2 Corinthians 6:4

Babies need lots of love! Have you ever helped care for a baby?

Saving Baby Moses

Exodus 1 – 2

A new king in Egypt feared the Israelites because there were so many of them. He thought they might try to take away his kingdom. So the king made the Israelites work as slaves. He also gave a terrible order: all new Israelite baby boys must be thrown into the Nile River to die!

Amram and Jochebed had a new baby boy. Jochebed kept him hidden for three months. When the baby was too big to hide any longer, she made a little basket and covered it with tar so it would float. Then she put her precious baby in the basket.

Near the king's palace, Jochebed hid the basket in tall grass at the river's edge. "Stay here," she told the baby's sister, Miriam. "Find out what happens."

An Egyptian princess came to the river and found the basket. When she opened it, the baby was crying. "He is one of the Israelite children!" said the princess.

Miriam thought quickly and hurried to the princess. "Should I find an Israelite woman to nurse the baby?" she asked.

"Yes," said the princess. Miriam ran and brought back Jochebed, the baby's own mother! "Take this baby home and nurse him for me," the princess said. Jochebed held her sweet baby close, thanking God for keeping him safe!

When the baby grew older, Jochebed brought him back to the princess. She adopted him as her son and named him Moses.

Sweet Thought
God watches over us!

Sweet Words
You keep me safe.
– Psalm 59:16

Doing new things and going new places can be lots of fun!

Good-bye, Egypt!

Exodus 3 – 12

The Israelites worked as slaves in Egypt for many years, but God knew how to rescue them. In the desert, from a fiery bush that did not burn up, God called to Moses.

"Go to Pharaoh, the king," God said. "Tell him that I say, 'Let my people go!'"

51

Moses obeyed, but Pharaoh laughed. "Ha! I will *not* let the people leave Egypt."

"Now I will send signs to Egypt to show Pharaoh my power," God told Moses.

First, God turned the water of the Nile River to yucky red. All the fish died and the river began to stink.

"No," said Pharaoh. "The people can't go."

Then God sent frogs hopping *everywhere*, even inside houses!

Pharaoh said no.

Next, swarms of gnats nibbled at everyone; then clouds of flies buzzed all around. Livestock got sick, and people got sores all over their bodies. God sent hail, lightning, and thunder. Hungry locusts gobbled crops in the fields and fruit on the trees.

Pharaoh still said no.

53

Then came darkness for three days. No one could see *anything*.

But stubborn Pharaoh would not let the people go. So God sent one last plague—a terrible sickness. Many Egyptians died, but the sickness passed over the Israelites.

Finally Pharaoh shouted, "Go!"

Quickly, Moses and God's people packed up and hurried out of Egypt.

Sweet Thought
God will make a way!

Sweet Words
Teach me how to follow you.
—Psalm 25:4

When good things happen, we want to celebrate!

Across the Red Sea

Exodus 14 – 15

$\mathcal{P}$haraoh, the king, was sorry he let the Israelites leave Egypt. He chased after them. In front of the Israelites was the sea, and behind them was Pharaoh's army. They were stuck!

"Don't be afraid!" Moses told the people. "The Lord will fight for you!"

That night, God put a cloud between Pharaoh's army and the Israelites. In the darkness, the army couldn't see at all, but the cloud gave the Israelites light.

"Now stretch out your hand over the sea," God told Moses, and Moses obeyed. With a strong wind, God opened up a path through the sea. The wind blew all night. The people walked across the sea on dry ground between walls of water!

Pharaoh's army started across the path through the sea, chasing the Israelites.

"Stretch out your hand over the sea," God told Moses again, and Moses obeyed. As the sun came up, the walls of water tumbled down on Pharaoh's army.

Moses and the people praised God with a song of joy because he rescued them and kept them safe. "There is no one else like you, God!" they sang. "You will lead and guide us with your love!" Then Moses' sister, Miriam, played a tambourine. She danced and sang with all the other women.

Sweet Thought
Great and wonderful is our God!

Sweet Words
Be glad and filled with joy.
– Psalm 68:3

What is your favorite food? Would you eat it every day?

A Sweet Treat Every Day

Exodus 16

The Israelites rubbed their rumbling tummies. What would they eat out here in the desert? "We're going to starve!" they cried to Moses.

God had a plan to take care of his people. A layer of dew fell all around the camp, leaving flakes like frost on the ground. "What is this?" the people wondered.

"This is food from God," said Moses. "He will send it each day. Gather what you need for one day only. Don't keep any extra."

The white flakes tasted like wafers made with sweet honey. Mmmm! The people called the flakes *manna*. They could bake it or boil it.

After everyone gathered manna for the day, the flakes melted away. Some people didn't listen to Moses and hid more manna than they needed in their tents. In the morning, it was rotten.

Then on the day before the Sabbath, God sent extra manna. "Today you may save some to eat tomorrow," Moses said. "The Sabbath is a day of rest. No manna will come tomorrow."

God sent manna to the people all the years they lived in the desert, until they entered the Promised Land.

Sweet Thought
God gives us what we
need each day.

Sweet Words
He gives food to
hungry people.
– Psalm 146:7

You're growing up when you start to take care of yourself!

God's Ten Rules

Exodus 19 – 20, 24, 31

God told Moses to tell the people, "If you obey God, you will be his treasure." The people promised to obey.

"Get ready to gather around the mountain," Moses said. "God wants to meet with you."

Bwaaaaaah! The people heard a loud trumpet blast. They saw smoke on the mountain. They followed Moses out of the camp and stood near the mountain.

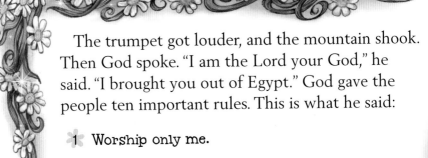

The trumpet got louder, and the mountain shook. Then God spoke. "I am the Lord your God," he said. "I brought you out of Egypt." God gave the people ten important rules. This is what he said:

1 Worship only me.

2 Don't make idols or worship them.

3 Respect my name.

4 Rest one day each week, because I rested after I made the world.

5 Honor your father and mother.

6 Don't kill people.

7 Always be faithful to your husband or wife.

8 Don't take what isn't yours.

9 Don't tell lies.

10 Don't be jealous of what someone else has.

The people listened. "We will obey God's rules," they said. "We will do what God wants."

Later, God told Moses to climb up the mountain. God wrote the ten rules on two stone tablets and gave them to Moses to take to the people.

Sweet Thought
God knows what is good for us.

Sweet Words
I will obey your word.
– Psalm 119:17

Everyone needs a place to belong.

Hide and Seek

Joshua 1 – 4, 6

"It's time to lead my people into the Promised Land," God told Joshua. "Be strong and brave. I am with you."

Joshua sent two spies to see the land and the city of Jericho with its tall, strong walls. A woman named Rahab hid the spies on the roof of her house.

Rahab wanted to know God. "Everyone here is afraid," she said. "We know what God has done for you. We know he rules over heaven and earth! Please let me and my family live when you come to take over our city."

"You have been kind to us," said the spies. "Keep this cord of red thread in your window. When our army comes, we will know this is your house. We will let you and your family live."

Rahab helped the spies get away before anyone in Jericho could find them. They climbed down the city wall using a rope. Then Rahab hung the red cord in her window.

When the Israelite army came to Jericho, the scouts found Rahab's house. They helped her and her family escape. The walls of Jericho tumbled down, but Rahab was safe among God's people.

Sweet Thought
God knows everyone's heart.

Sweet Words
When you look for me with all your heart, you will find me.

–Jeremiah 29:13

Something new might be hard, but you can do it!

Deborah Leads the Army

Judges 4 – 5

Deborah, a leader in Israel, loved God and trusted him. The Israelites had not been obeying God, so the evil king of Canaan ruled over them. But when the people cried to God to help them, he did. He told Deborah what to do.

Deborah called for a man named Barak. "God has a job for you," she said. "Gather an army of ten thousand men. Go to Mount Tabor to fight the Canaanites. God will help you."

Barak was afraid. He wanted to be sure he had God's help. He said to Deborah, "If you go with me into battle, I will go."

"I will go with you," said Deborah.

Deborah went with Barak to his hometown. He called for men to join his army. She went with the army to Mount Tabor. Then at the right time for the battle, she told Barak, "Get ready and go! This is the day! God is going ahead of you."

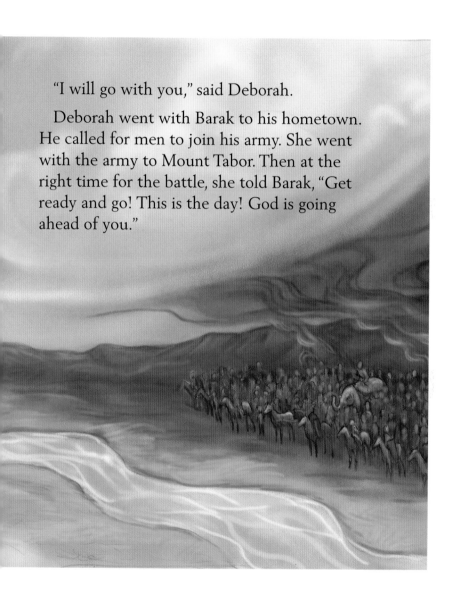

Deborah spoke the truth. God fought for Barak's army when they attacked the Canaanites. The Canaanite leader ran away. With Deborah by his side, Barak and his army chased all the Canaanite chariots. They won the battle. Deborah and Barak sang a victory song.

Sweet Thought
God helps us with
hard tasks.

Sweet Words
You give me strength.
– *Psalm 18:1*

Who is your best friend?

Ruth's Reward

The Book of Ruth

Ruth stood on the dusty road with her sister-in-law Orpah and her mother-in-law, Naomi. The women cried together. Naomi, an Israelite, was going back to her home in Bethlehem.

"I will miss you greatly, dear ones," said Naomi, "but you must return to your mothers' households."

Orpah kissed Naomi good-bye, but Ruth would not leave her. Ruth trusted God. "I will go wherever you go," she told Naomi. "Your people will be my people, and your God will be my God."

82

Ruth traveled with Naomi all the way to Bethlehem. They found a place to live. Ruth worked in the barley fields and walked behind the harvest workers, gathering loose stalks of grain that fell on the ground. She took the stalks home, and Naomi baked bread with the grain.

Naomi's relative Boaz owned the fields. "Who is that young woman?" Boaz asked his workers.

"Her name is Ruth," they told him.

Boaz knew about Ruth's kindness to Naomi. "Be sure that no one harms Ruth," he said, "and leave extra grain for her to gather."

"How exciting!" said Naomi when she heard about Boaz. She guessed what would happen next.

Boaz and Ruth got married! Then they had a baby boy—Obed, grandfather of the great King David.

Sweet Thought
God notices when we rely on him!

Sweet Words
The Lord will give you a reward.
– Ephesians 6:8

What could be better than hearing your favorite bedtime story!

What Samuel Heard

1 Samuel 1, 3

Hannah cried quietly as she prayed, "Lord, please let me have a baby. If you do, he will serve you all his life." God gave Hannah a baby boy. She named him Samuel.

When Samuel was old enough, he helped Eli, the priest at the beautiful tent where people worshiped God.

One night at bedtime, Samuel heard his name. He thought Eli was calling him. "I'm coming!" said Samuel. He ran to see what Eli wanted.

"I didn't call you," Eli said. "Go back to bed."

Samuel obeyed Eli, but he heard his name again—"Samuel!" He got up and went to Eli. "Here I am," he told Eli. "Did you call me?"

"I didn't call you," Eli said. "Go back to bed."

Samuel went back to bed, but he heard his name again—"Samuel!" He got up and went to Eli. Now Eli understood that God was calling Samuel.

90

"Go back to bed," said Eli. "If someone calls again, say, 'Speak, Lord. Your servant is listening.'"

"Samuel!" God called again!

"Speak, Lord," said Samuel. "I'm listening."

God gave Samuel a message for Eli. After that, Samuel became God's messenger to the people of Israel. He served God his entire life, just as Hannah had prayed.

Sweet Thought
God speaks to us!

Sweet Words
You gave me ears
to hear you.
– Psalm 40:6

Sheep never worry when their shepherd is nearby.

David, the Shepherd King

1 Samuel 16 – 17; Psalm 23

God sent Samuel to Bethlehem. "Invite Jesse and his sons to dinner," God said. "One of Jesse's sons will be the next king."

When Samuel saw Jesse's oldest son, he thought, *This must be the one!* But God told Samuel, "He's not the one."

Samuel counted Jesse's sons—one, two, three, four, five, six, seven. None of them was the one God had chosen. "Do you have another son?" Samuel asked.

"One more," said Jesse. "He's out in the fields, watching my sheep."

"Send for him," said Samuel. "We can't eat until he comes."

David lovingly cared for Jesse's sheep. He found sweet green grass for them to eat and brooks with clean water to drink. He counted the sheep to be sure none got lost. When the sheep rested, David played his harp. He wrote songs about God's wonderful love. David was a gentle shepherd.

But David was brave too. Sometimes hungry bears and lions came near, looking for a lamb to eat. David fought off the bears and lions with his staff!

When David arrived for dinner, God told Samuel, "This is the one." Samuel poured oil on David's head. David would be Israel's next king!

Sweet Thought
God cares for his people.

Sweet Words
The Lord is my shepherd.
– Psalm 23:1

If you could ask for any gift, what would it be?

Wise King Solomon

1 Kings 3 – 4, 10

When Solomon became king of Israel, he wondered if he would be a good king like his father, David. Solomon worshiped God at a place called Gibeon. One night God came to Solomon in a dream.

"What do you want, Solomon?" called God. "Ask, and I will give it to you."

Oh, my! Solomon could ask for anything he wanted. What should he choose? Riches? Honor? A long life?

"Help me lead your people," said Solomon. "Give me understanding to know right from wrong." Solomon asked God for *wisdom*.

"I am happy with you, Solomon," God said. "You didn't ask for anything for yourself. You asked for help to be a good king. I will give you what you asked for! You will be the wisest man who ever lived. I also will give you what you did *not* ask for—money and honor. No other king will be like you. And if you follow and obey me like your father David did, I will give you a long life too."

God did what he promised. Wise, rich, and famous, King Solomon ruled God's people well for many happy years.

Sweet Thought
God teaches us
what is right.

Sweet Words
The Lord gives wisdom.
—Proverbs 2:6

When you play dress-up, what do you pretend to be?

Brave Queen Esther

The Book of Esther

Beautiful Esther, a young Jewish girl, became the queen of Persia. She loved to wear shimmery gowns and sparkly jewelry for her husband, the king.

But being queen could be difficult too. One of the king's helpers tricked the king into making a bad law. It hurt the Jewish people. The king didn't know that Esther was Jewish!

Then a messenger came to Esther with words from
her cousin Mordecai: "Esther, you must go to the king
and plead with him. You must help your people."

"But no one may see the king without being invited
first," Esther replied. "Unless the king holds out his
golden scepter to welcome me, I could die!"

Another message came from Mordecai: "Perhaps
you became queen for a time like this—to save your
people!"

Brave Queen Esther agreed to go to the king. She put on her royal robes and entered the king's throne room. The king held out his golden scepter—Esther would not die!

She invited the king to dinner. There she said, "Your law to hurt the Jewish people will hurt me too, because I am a Jew."

Upset to hear what he had done, the king agreed to help the Jews, not hurt them. Esther's brave choice helped to save her people!

Sweet Thought
God has a plan for your life!

Sweet Words
God is working in you.
– Philippians 2:13

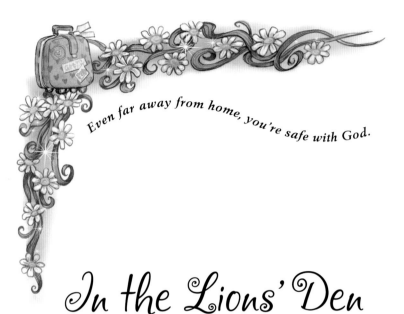

Even far away from home, you're safe with God.

In the Lions' Den

Daniel 1, 6

*D*aniel lived in Babylon, far from his home in Judah. But Daniel wasn't afraid. He trusted God, and Daniel earned a high position, helping to rule the kingdom.

Then a new king made a law. No one should pray to anyone but him, or else they would be eaten by hungry lions!

Judah   Lions' Den   Babylon

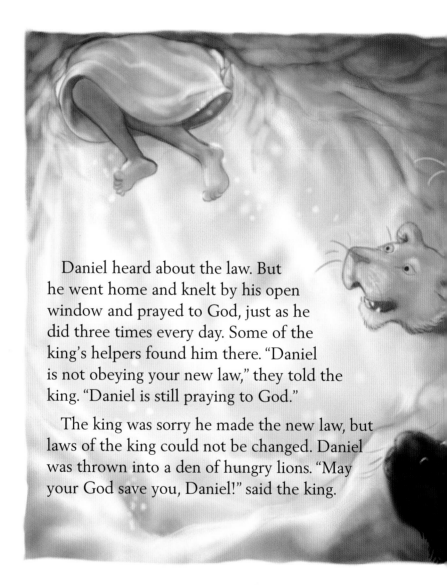

Daniel heard about the law. But he went home and knelt by his open window and prayed to God, just as he did three times every day. Some of the king's helpers found him there. "Daniel is not obeying your new law," they told the king. "Daniel is still praying to God."

The king was sorry he made the new law, but laws of the king could not be changed. Daniel was thrown into a den of hungry lions. "May your God save you, Daniel!" said the king.

In the morning, the king rushed to the lions' den. "Daniel!" he shouted. "Did your God save you?"

"Yes!" called Daniel. "God sent an angel to shut the lions' mouths. The lions did not hurt me!"

The king made another new law: "Everyone should worship Daniel's God. He is strong and powerful and rescued Daniel from the lions."

Sweet Thought
God protects us when we trust him.

Sweet Words
We trust in the Lord our God.
– Psalm 20:7

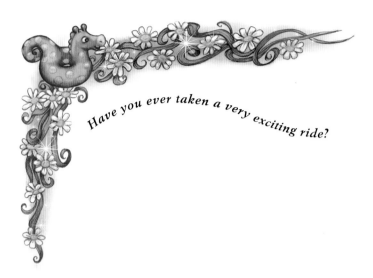

Have you ever taken a very exciting ride?

Jonah's Wild Ride

Jonah 1 – 3

"Jonah, go to Nineveh," God said. "Tell the people to stop doing wrong and start doing right. Otherwise I must punish them."

Jonah didn't want to obey God. He didn't want God to care about the bad people of Nineveh. So Jonah boarded a ship sailing *away* from Nineveh.

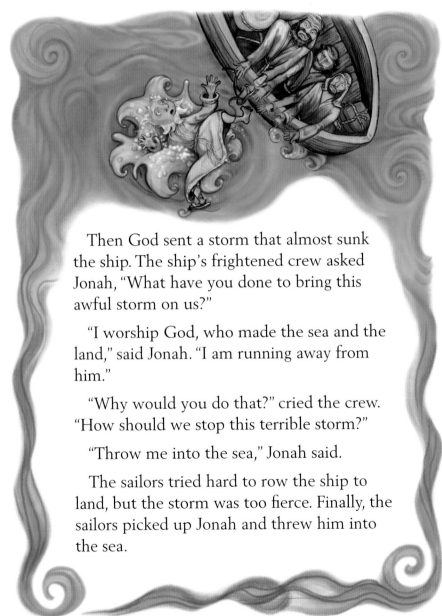

Then God sent a storm that almost sunk the ship. The ship's frightened crew asked Jonah, "What have you done to bring this awful storm on us?"

"I worship God, who made the sea and the land," said Jonah. "I am running away from him."

"Why would you do that?" cried the crew. "How should we stop this terrible storm?"

"Throw me into the sea," Jonah said.

The sailors tried hard to row the ship to land, but the storm was too fierce. Finally, the sailors picked up Jonah and threw him into the sea.

The storm stopped!

God sent a huge fish to swallow Jonah and keep him safe. For three days and nights, Jonah thought about what he had done.

He prayed to God and said he was sorry. God told the fish to spit Jonah out on the beach.

"Go to Nineveh," God said again. This time Jonah obeyed God, and the people of Nineveh did too!

Sweet Thought
God will rescue us!

Sweet Words
The Lord has made known
his power to save.
–Psalm 98:2

New Testament

Jesus said, "Let the little children come to me.
Don't keep them away. The kingdom of heaven
belongs to people like them."

–Matthew 19:14

What's the biggest surprise you've ever had?

A Message for Mary

Luke 1

In the town of Nazareth lived a young woman named Mary. She was engaged to marry a man named Joseph when God sent the angel Gabriel to her with a message.

"Hello, Mary," said the angel. "God is pleased with you, and he is with you."

What could the angel mean? Mary didn't know.

"Don't be afraid, Mary," the angel said. "God has a wonderful surprise for you. You are going to have a baby! Give him the name Jesus. The baby will be God's Son. God will make him a king like David. He will lead God's people forever."

"I don't understand," said Mary. "How can I have a baby? I'm not married yet."

"God will make this happen," said the angel. "Nothing is impossible with God."

"I serve the Lord," Mary said. "Whatever God wants, I will do."

The angel went away. Mary hurried to the hill country to visit her relative Elizabeth. "Hello, Elizabeth!" she called as she went inside the house.

God told Elizabeth about Mary's baby. "What a wonderful surprise!" Elizabeth exclaimed. "What joyful news!"

Then Mary praised God for all his goodness. "He has done great things!" she said.

Sweet Thought
God does wonderful things!

Sweet Words
A child will be born to us.
– Isaiah 9:6

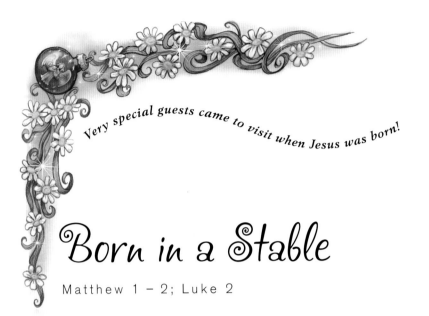

Very special guests came to visit when Jesus was born!

Born in a Stable

Matthew 1 – 2; Luke 2

Mary and Joseph traveled to Bethlehem. There were no guest rooms in the crowded city when they arrived, so they found a stable where they could sleep on the hay.

That night in the stable, baby Jesus was born! Mary wrapped him in swaddling clothes and laid him in a manger.

Out in the fields, sleepy shepherds guarding their sheep suddenly opened their eyes and blinked. Brilliant light shone all around! An angel said to the shepherds, "Don't be afraid. I have good news! Tonight in Bethlehem your Savior is born! You will find him wrapped in swaddling clothes and lying in a manger."

Then the whole sky filled up with angels praising
God. "Glory to God and peace to those who please
him!" they said.

The shepherds hurried into Bethlehem and found
Mary, Joseph, and baby Jesus, just as the angel told
them.

Far away in the East, wise men saw a new star in the sky. "It's the star of the new king of Israel!" they said. "We must go and worship him." They loaded their camels with gifts of gold, frankincense, and myrrh and set out on a long trip across the desert. When they arrived in Bethlehem and found the house where Jesus was, the wise men knelt to honor the child and gave him all their gifts.

Sweet Thought
We can all know Jesus!

Sweet Words
A king will rise up out of Israel.
– Numbers 24:17

131

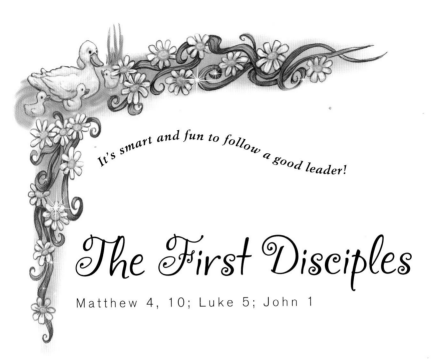

It's smart and fun to follow a good leader!

The First Disciples

Matthew 4, 10; Luke 5; John 1

As Jesus grew up, so did John the Baptist, the son of Mary's relative Elizabeth. John the Baptist told people to get ready for Jesus.

One day as Jesus walked by, John the Baptist said, "Look! The Lamb of God!"

A man named Andrew heard what John said. He called to Jesus, "Teacher! Where are you staying?" Andrew wanted to talk with Jesus.

"Come, and you will see," said Jesus. Andrew followed Jesus and talked with him. The next day Andrew brought his brother Peter to meet Jesus too!

JESUS   JOHN

As Jesus traveled to another town, he met Philip. "Follow me," said Jesus. Then Philip brought his friend Nathanael to meet Jesus.

Jesus saw Andrew and Peter again, throwing a fishing net into the sea. "Come, follow me!" called Jesus. "I will teach you how to fish for people!" Peter and Andrew left their boat and followed Jesus. Then Jesus called James and John, who joined him too.

Jesus met a tax collector named Matthew. "Come, follow me!" said Jesus.

Later Jesus went up a mountain and prayed to God all night. In the morning he chose twelve special helpers: Peter and Andrew, James and John, Philip and Bartholomew, Thomas and Matthew, another man named James, plus Thaddeus, Simon, and Judas.

Sweet Thought
Jesus wants everyone to follow him.

Sweet Words
Go and make disciples of all nations.
– Matthew 28:19

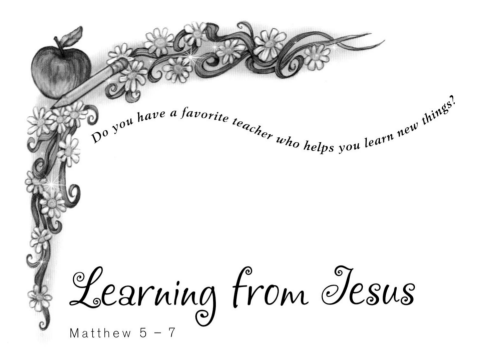

Do you have a favorite teacher who helps you learn new things?

Learning from Jesus

Matthew 5 – 7

Jesus walked up a mountainside and sat down. People gathered around, and Jesus taught them.

"God blesses you when you depend on him," Jesus said. "That's when his kingdom belongs to you. Love other people, and always be kind—even to those who hurt you."

Jesus taught about helping others. "Give to those in need," he said, "but make it a secret between God and you. Don't give to others to get praise for yourself."

Jesus taught about money. "Use your money well," he said. "Don't spend it all on yourself. If you love God, you can't love money too. Don't worry about tomorrow. God takes care of you day by day."

Jesus taught a special rule, the Golden Rule: "Do for others what you would want them to do for you," he said. "This matters to God."

Then Jesus told a story about a man who built his house on a sturdy rock and another man who built his house on sand. Wind, rain, and waves beat on both houses when storms came. The house built on sand fell down, but the house built on rock stood strong. "If you listen to me and obey my words," said Jesus, "you'll be like the man who built *that* house."

Sweet Thought

Jesus teaches us.

Sweet Words

Let Christ's word live in you
like a rich treasure.

– Colossians 3:16

Bubble baths and lotion keep us clean and sweet!

A New Start

Luke 7

At Simon's house, a woman saw Jesus eating dinner with Simon and his guests. Oh, how she wanted God to forgive her and help her stop doing the bad things she always did! She wanted a new life.

Carrying a lovely alabaster jar filled with expensive perfume, the woman walked straight to Jesus and stood behind him. She was so sorry for all her sins. And somehow Jesus knew that, she felt sure.

141

The woman began to cry. Her tears fell on Jesus' feet, getting them wet. She used her long hair to wipe the tears away. Then she poured the perfume from the jar on Jesus' feet.

All the dinner guests stopped talking.

Jesus said, "Simon, when I came to your house tonight, you gave me no water to wash the dust off my feet. This woman washed my feet with her tears and dried them with her hair. You gave me no oil for my head, but this woman poured perfume on my feet. When a person is forgiven of much, like this woman, she shows much love."

Then Jesus told the woman, "You are forgiven. Go your way in peace."

What a reason to smile! Jesus gave the woman a new start!

Sweet Thought
Jesus gives us new life!

Sweet Words
Forgive, just as the Lord forgave you.
– Colossians 3:13

When scary things happen, we need someone to help us feel safe.

Calming the Storm

Mark 4; Luke 8

Jesus and his disciples got into a boat and headed to the other side of the lake. Tired, Jesus lay down in the boat and fell asleep on a cushion.

Quietly the disciples rowed—*push-pull, push-pull.*

Suddenly the wind puffed wildly all around. "Hey, what's happening?" yelled the disciples. "Where did this storm come from? Row harder!"

The waves on the lake swelled and hit the sides of the boat. The wind whooshed and howled.

The waves grew bigger, crashing over the little boat and filling it with water. "We're starting to sink!" the disciples shouted. "What are we going to do?"

Despite the storm, Jesus kept sleeping. The disciples gathered around him. "Master!" they shouted. "Help us! We're going to drown!"

Jesus woke up. He heard the wind and saw the waves. "Why are you afraid?" he asked the disciples. "Be quiet," he told the wind, and the wind hushed. "Settle down," he told the waves, and right away the waves stopped.

The disciples didn't know what to think. Even the wind and the waves obeyed Jesus!

Sweet Thought
Jesus is strong and powerful!

Sweet Words
I am always with you.
– Matthew 28:20

It's good to have someone help us when we're sick.

A Woman's Faith

Mark 5; Luke 8

Jesus walked down a road, surrounded by a crowd. Everyone wanted to see him—especially a woman who had been sick for twelve long years. She wanted to be well, but no doctors could help her.

If I just touch Jesus' clothes, thought the woman, *I will get well.* She edged up through the crowd close to Jesus and touched the edge of his robe. Instantly she felt the sickness leave!

Jesus stopped and turned around. "Who touched me?" he asked.

"Look at all these people, Lord!" said the disciples. "They all keep bumping into you. How can you say, 'Who touched me?'"

"Someone touched me on purpose," said Jesus.

The woman trembled. Jesus knew what she had done. She knelt at Jesus' feet and told him the whole truth. "I'm the one who touched you," she said. "I have been so sick. I wanted to be well. I thought if I just touched your clothes, I would be healed. And now I'm well!"

Jesus smiled at the woman. "Your faith has healed you," he said. "Your sickness is gone. Don't be afraid, and go in peace."

Sweet Thought
Jesus makes us well.

Sweet Words
He heals all my sicknesses.
– Psalm 103:3

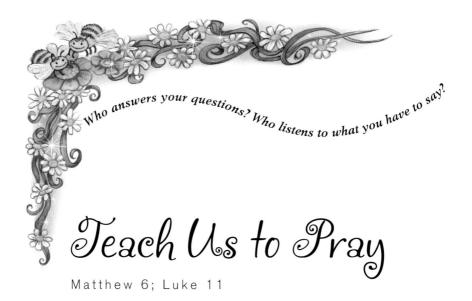

Who answers your questions? Who listens to what you have to say?

Teach Us to Pray

Matthew 6; Luke 11

$\mathcal{J}$esus loved to pray to God. Once, as he finished praying, one of his disciples said, "Lord, teach us to pray."

Then Jesus taught his friends more about praying. "Don't give up," he said. "Never stop praying. God listens to you, and he will answer. Keep asking, and you will receive. Keep looking, and you will find. Keep knocking, and the door will open. Your heavenly Father is good, and he will give good gifts to you. He will give you the Holy Spirit."

Jesus said to them, "When you pray, this is what you should say.

'Father, may your name be honored.

May your kingdom come.

Give us each day our daily bread.

Forgive us our sins,

as we also forgive everyone

who sins against us.

Keep us from falling into sin when

we are tempted.'"

Sweet Thought
God hears and answers when we pray.

Sweet Words
I will listen to you.
– Jeremiah 29:12

Have you ever lost something important and then found it again?

Lost and Found

Luke 15

Jesus told this story:

A father had two sons. The younger son asked his father for money, left home, and traveled far away. He wasted his money doing bad things. When the money was gone and the son was hungry, he got a job feeding pigs.

He was so hungry he wanted to eat the pigs' food!

Finally he came to his senses. "My father's servants have plenty to eat," he said. "I will go home to my father. I will tell him I'm sorry for what I've done. I don't deserve to be his son, but I will ask my father to make me his servant."

So the young man started the journey home.

The father, hoping his lost son would come back someday, often watched for him. When he spotted the young man traveling toward home, his son was still a long way off. The father ran to him, hugged him, and kissed him!

"Father, I'm sorry for the wrong things I've done," said the young man. "I'm not worthy to be your son."

But the father said, "Quick! Bring my son the best clothes in the house! Get him a ring and sandals for his feet! We must celebrate! My son was lost and now he's found!"

The father's older son refused to come to the party. "I've always obeyed you," he told his father, "but you've never had a celebration for me."

162

"You have always been here with me," said the father, "and everything I have is yours. We must celebrate and be glad now because my son who was lost has been found!"

Sweet Thought
God forgives us when we turn to him.

Sweet Words
You always show me the path that leads to life.
– Psalm 16:11

When someone we love is glad to see us, we feel glad too!

Let the Children Come

Matthew 19; Mark 10; Luke 18

Some mothers and fathers wanted Jesus to bless their little children. So they took a walk and found him. "We want to see Jesus," they told his disciples. "We want him to put his hands on our children and pray for them."

"Jesus doesn't have time for *that*!" said the disciples. "He can't stop what he's doing just to spend time with children. Can't you see how busy he is? Move along now, and take these children home!"

With sad faces, the mothers and fathers and little children slowly walked away.

But then they heard a voice calling, "Children, come back!" The mothers stopped and turned around. The fathers stopped and turned around. The little children stopped and turned around. Who could be calling them? Hurray! It was Jesus!

"Let the little children come to me!" Jesus told his disciples. "Don't stop them! They are important in God's kingdom. They are important to me."

Then Jesus hugged the little boys and girls and blessed each one.

Sweet Thought
You are important to Jesus!

Sweet Words
He cares about you.
— 1 Peter 5:7

Shout hurray and strike up the band!

A Big Parade

Mark 11; John 12

On the way to Jerusalem with his disciples, Jesus gave two disciples an errand. "Go to the village up ahead," he said. "You will find a donkey colt. Bring him back to me."

The disciples found the donkey, brought him to Jesus, and spread their coats over his back. Jesus sat on the donkey and rode toward the city of Jerusalem.

"Hosanna! Our King is coming!" people shouted along the way. They threw their coats on the road in front of Jesus. They cut down leafy tree branches and spread those on the road ahead of him too.

Inside Jerusalem, people heard that Jesus was on his way to the city. They took palm branches and hurried out to meet him. When they went out of the city gates, they saw Jesus riding toward them on the donkey.

What a big parade, with Jesus in the middle!

People behind him, people beside him, and people ahead of him all walked together toward the city, shouting, "Hosanna, praise God! He sent us Jesus, our King!"

Sweet Thought
Jesus is our King!

Sweet Words
Our hearts are full of joy because of him.
– Psalm 33:21

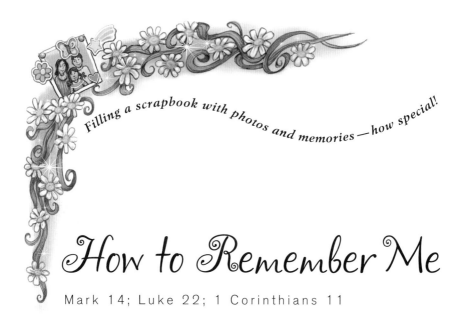

How to Remember Me

Mark 14; Luke 22; 1 Corinthians 11

Jesus and his disciples ate a special meal together at Passover, a time to remember how God brought his people out of Egypt.

"Where do you want us to prepare our Passover supper?" the disciples asked Jesus.

"Go into the city," Jesus told Peter and John. "You will see a man carrying a water pitcher. Follow him to a house. The owner of the house will take you upstairs to a large room. That's where we will eat." Peter and John did as Jesus told them and prepared the meal.

That night, Jesus came and sat at the table with his disciples. As they were eating, he held one of the loaves of bread and thanked God for it. Then he broke the bread into pieces and gave them to his friends.

"Eat this," Jesus said. "This is my body. It is given for you. Every time you eat it, do it in memory of me."

Then Jesus took a cup of wine and thanked God for it. "Drink this," Jesus said. "This cup is the new covenant in my blood. Every time you drink it, do it in memory of me."

After supper, Jesus and his friends sang a song and walked outside together to a garden called Gethsemane.

Sweet Thought
Jesus wants us to remember him.

Sweet Words
I am the way and the truth and the life.
–John 14:6

What do you do when you feel sad?

The Saddest Day

Matthew 26 – 27; Luke 23; John 19

Jesus never did anything wrong, not even one little thing! But some leaders of God's people did not want Jesus to be their king.

The leaders sent men to arrest Jesus in the garden of Gethsemane. Jesus could have stopped them, but he didn't. He knew this was part of God's plan.

Jesus' disciples all ran away.

The leaders hit Jesus and spit on him. They took him to the governor. They wanted Jesus to die. Some other people did too. "Crucify him!" everyone shouted.

The governor let the leaders and shouting people have their way. He handed Jesus over to his soldiers to die on a cross.

The soldiers made fun of Jesus and put a crown of sharp thorns on his head. They made Jesus carry a heavy cross out of the city. They nailed Jesus' hands and feet to the cross.

"Father, forgive them," Jesus said. "They don't know what they are doing." A little later Jesus said, "It is finished." Then he died.

A man named Joseph buried Jesus' body in a hillside tomb cut in the rock, like a cave. Joseph closed the tomb with a large, heavy stone and slowly walked away.

Sweet Thought
Jesus died for our sins!

Sweet Words
He will forgive every wrong thing we have done.
– 1 John 1:9

In spring there is new life all around us!

Alive Again!

Matthew 28; Luke 24

On the Sunday morning after Jesus died, some women walked to Jesus' tomb. They wanted to put spices and ointments on Jesus' body.

"How will we get in?" they wondered. "Who will move the stone?"

But when they arrived, the tomb was open—the stone was rolled away! The women walked inside. Where was Jesus' body? They couldn't find him anywhere.

Suddenly two dazzling angels spoke to them. "Why are you looking for Jesus here?" the angels asked. "He isn't here. He has risen! Remember what he told you—that he would die but rise again! Now go and tell his disciples he is alive. He is going ahead of you to Galilee, and you will see him there."

Trembling but full of joy, the women ran from the tomb. They rushed back into the city to find the disciples and give them the angels' message.

And on their way, they saw Jesus! They ran to him and worshiped him. "Don't be afraid," he said. "Go now and tell my disciples to go to Galilee, and they will see me there."

Sweet Thought
Jesus is alive!

Sweet Words
Christ has been raised
from the dead.
– Romans 6:4

How strong are you? Show me a muscle!

Wind and Fire

Acts 1 – 2

After his resurrection, Jesus appeared to his friends for forty days. One day he told his disciples, "Wait here in Jerusalem; don't leave the city. You will receive power when the Holy Spirit comes. You will tell people everywhere about me."

Then Jesus left his friends and went up into heaven. The disciples stayed together and waited, as Jesus told them to do.

When all the believers were together, suddenly the sound of a roaring wind filled the house where they were meeting. Flames of fire came and rested on each person. The Holy Spirit filled all the believers, and they began to speak in other languages that they had never learned!

Visitors from far away heard the commotion and hurried to see what was going on. "This is amazing!" the visitors said. "These men are praising God in our own languages! What can this mean?"

The Holy Spirit gave Peter courage. "Listen, friends!" Peter shouted. "This happened because God has sent his Holy Spirit. He promised to do this, just as he promised to send us a Savior. Jesus is the Savior!"

The people listened while Peter told them about Jesus, and nearly three thousand people believed and were baptized that day!

Sweet Thought
The Holy Spirit makes us strong with his power!

Sweet Words
Be filled with the Holy Spirit.
−Ephesians 5:18

Saul Meets Jesus

Acts 9, 22, 26

S aul did not believe Jesus was God's Son. He did not believe Jesus rose from the dead. Saul did whatever he could to hurt and scare Jesus' followers.

But as Saul traveled to the city of Damascus, bright light suddenly flashed around him, and he fell down. A voice said, "Saul! Saul! Why are you hurting me?"

"Who are you, sir?" asked Saul.

"I am Jesus," said the voice. "Now get up and go into the city. There you will learn what you must do." Saul had been wrong—Jesus was alive!

When Saul got up, he couldn't see. His friends led him by the hand into the city. Saul waited there three days.

Then Jesus told a man named Ananias, "Go to Saul and lay hands on him so he can see again. I have chosen Saul to tell many people about me."

Ananias came to Saul. He placed his hands on Saul and said, "Brother Saul, you met Jesus on the road. He has sent me. You will be able to see again, and you will be filled with the Holy Spirit." Immediately, Saul could see! He got up and was baptized right away. He would follow Jesus for the rest of his life.

Sweet Thought
Jesus wants us to know him.

Sweet Words
I know the One I
have believed in.
– 2 Timothy 1:12

We can read about God's power and great love!

Joining the Journey

Acts 16; 2 Timothy 1, 3

S aul had a new name—Paul. He had a new job too—going from place to place to preach about Jesus and help the believers.

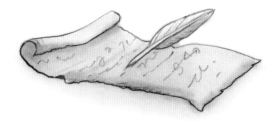

PAUL

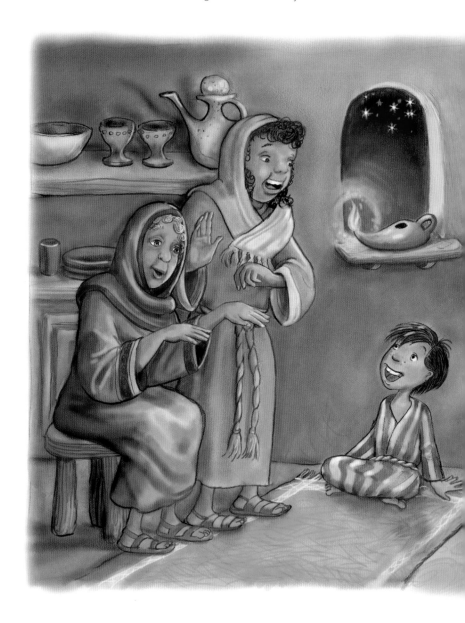

On one of his trips, Paul met Timothy, his mother, and his grandmother. Eunice and Lois loved God's Word. Timothy first learned about God through them. He learned about God the creator. He heard God's promises to Abraham, Isaac, and Jacob. He learned how God led his people out of Egypt and into the Promised Land. He learned about King David and about the King who was to come.

When Timothy learned to read, he could read God's Word himself. He read what God says is right and what is wrong. He read about God's power and his great love.

Timothy grew wise by knowing God's Word. When Eunice and Lois talked about Jesus, Timothy knew they were telling the truth: Jesus is our Savior and the King who was to come!

All the believers in Timothy's town thought well of Timothy and wanted Paul to meet him. Paul could see Timothy's faith, and Paul said, "Timothy, join me on my journey." So Timothy traveled with Paul to visit other churches. Even though he was young, he helped Paul in a big way!

Sweet Thought
God's Word points us
to Jesus.

Sweet Words
Your word is truth
– John 17:17

A New Believer

Acts 16

Paul and his friend Silas boarded a boat and sailed for Macedonia, where God wanted them to tell people the good news about Jesus. After they reached land, they went to the city of Philippi.

They walked outside the city gates to look for people who had gathered to pray. They found a group of women near the riverbank and sat down to talk with them. One of the women was Lydia, a merchant who sold expensive cloth.

Lydia worshiped God, but she had not heard the good news of Jesus. She listened carefully to everything Paul said. Jesus died on the cross and rose again! Jesus could forgive her sins! God helped Lydia understand that what Paul said was true. What good news! Lydia believed in Jesus, and she was baptized, along with others in her household.

Happy and thankful, Lydia said to Paul and Silas, "Please stay at my house while you are in our city, if you think I am a believer in the Lord." So until it was time for them to go on to another place, Paul and Silas stayed at Lydia's house while they preached about Jesus in Philippi.

Sweet Thought
The good news is for everyone!

Sweet Words
How beautiful are ... those who bring good news!
– Romans 10:15

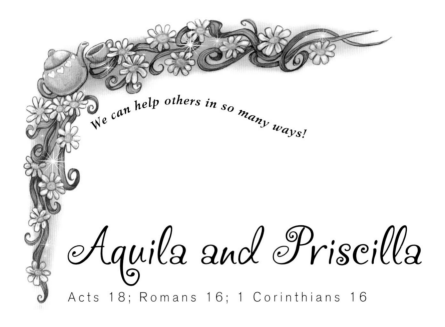

We can help others in so many ways!

Aquila and Priscilla

Acts 18; Romans 16; 1 Corinthians 16

When Paul came to the city of Corinth, he met Aquila and his wife, Priscilla—believers who earned money by making tents. Paul also made tents, so he stayed with Aquila and Priscilla in their house and worked with them.

Aquila and Priscilla served Jesus together. They served Jesus by helping Paul. They sailed with him to Ephesus. Aquila and Priscilla settled there, but Paul continued on his journey. Later Paul came back to visit. He was glad to see his friends again and all the believers who met in their house for church.

213

Aquila and Priscilla served Jesus by being kind. Instead of embarrassing a man named Apollos by correcting him in front of others, they waited to speak with him alone. "Let us tell you more about Jesus' teaching," they said. Apollos was happy to learn from such kind friends.

Aquila and Priscilla kept serving Jesus when they moved to Rome. They used their house as a meeting place for the church there too. "Greet Priscilla and Aquila, my fellow workers in Christ Jesus," Paul wrote to the church in Rome. "They helped me so much, and all the churches here are thankful."

Sweet Thought
We serve Jesus when we help others.

Sweet Words
Serve one another in love.
– Galatians 5:13

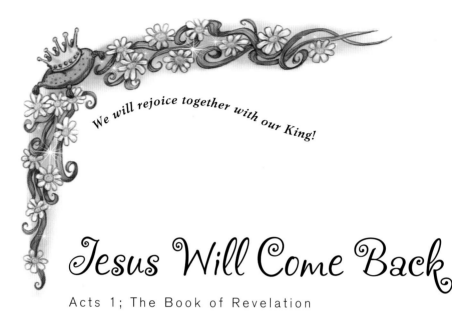

We will rejoice together with our King!

Jesus Will Come Back

Acts 1; The Book of Revelation

After Jesus rose again, he took his disciples up on a mountain. As his friends watched, Jesus went up into heaven through the clouds.

The disciples kept looking up, wishing they could still see Jesus. Then two angels came and said, "Why are you staring at the sky? Jesus has gone into heaven. But someday he will come back, just as you saw him go!"

Many years later Jesus gave a vision to John, one of Jesus' disciples. "Write down what you see," said Jesus.

In the vision, John saw Jesus dressed in a white robe with a gold sash and shining brightly like the sun.

And John saw heaven, with angels around God's throne, and every creature in heaven and on earth sang praises to God and Jesus.

And John saw a beautiful new heavenly city, sparkling like jewels, where God will live with his people forever after Jesus comes back.

"He will come with the clouds of heaven," John wrote, "and everyone will see him."

"I am coming soon," said Jesus. "I am the First and Last, the Beginning and the End."

We are waiting for you, Lord Jesus!

Sweet Thought
We will see Jesus!

Sweet Words
Every eye will see him.
– Revelation 1:7